MW01094771

ISBN 0-933546-54-8

9 780933 546547 >

KHANIQAHI NIMATULLAHI
(CENTERS OF THE NIMATULLAHI SUFI ORDER)

306 West 11th Street
New York, New York 10014
Tel: 212-924-7739
Fax: 212-924-5479

4021 19th Avenue
San Francisco,
California 94132
Tel: 415-586-1313

4931 MacArthur Blvd. NW
Washington D.C. 20007
Tel: 202-338-4757

84 Pembroke Street
Boston Massachusetts 02118
Tel: 617-536-0076

310 NE 57th Street
Seattle,
Washington 98105
Tel: 206-527-5018

11019 Arleta Avenue
Mission Hills,
Los Angeles,
California 91345
Tel: 818-365-2226

4642 North Hermitage
Chicago, Illinois 60640
Tel:312-561-1616

405 Greg Avenue
Santa Fe,
New Mexico 87501
Tel: 505-983-8500

219 Chace Street
Santa Cruz,
California 95060
Tel: 408-425-8454

95 Old Lansdowne Road
West Didsbury,
Manchester
M20 8NZ, United Kingdom
Tel: 061-434-8857

Kölnerstrasse 176
5000 Köln 90 (Porz)
Federal Republic of Germany
Tel: 49-2203-15390

50 Rue du 4eme Zouaves
Rosny-sous-Bois
Paris, 93110 France
Tel: 48552809

63 Boulevard Latrille
BP 1224 Abidjan
CIDEX 1 Côte d'Ivoire, Africa
Tel: 225-410510

87A Mullens Street
Balmain, Sydney, Australia 2041
Tel: 612-555-7546

Viale Liberazione, 1
Vaiano Cremasco (CR)
Milan, Italy
Tel: 39-373-277-246

C/Abedul 11
Madrid 28036
Spain
Tel:341-350-2086

41 Chepstow Place
London W2 4TS
United Kingdom
Tel: 071-229-0769
Fax: 071-221-7025

Nightingales Under the Snow

Poems by

Annemarie Schimmel

Foreword by Dr. Javad Nurbakhsh

Khaniqahi Nimatullahi Publications
London & New York

Calligraphy on the cover by Dr. Shams Anvari

Illustration courtesey of British Library
MS period OR period 7573

Printed in the United Kingdom
on acid free paper.

British Library Cataloging in publication data

Nightingales Under the Snow
Poems by Annemarie Schimmel

I. Annemarie Schimmel

ISBN 0-933546-54-8

First British Edition published 1994 by KNP
41 Chepstow Place
London W2 4TS
England

Tel: 071-229-0769
Fax: 071-221-7025

Dedication

MAULANA'S LAST LETTER TO SHAMS

Sometimes I wonder, sweetest love, if you
Were a mere dream in a long winter night,
A dream of spring-days, and of golden light
Which sheds its rays upon a frozen heart;
A dream of wine that fills the drunken eye.

And so I wonder, sweetest love, if I
Should drink this ruby wine, or rather weep:
Each tear a bezel with your face engraved,
A rosary to memorize your name...

There are so many ways to call you back —
Yes, even if you only were a dream.

Contents

New England

Journeys

The Great Mughals

Sufi Shrines

Impressions from India

Songs from Sind

Foreword

Annemarie Schimmel is former Professor of the History of Religion in the Faculty of Islamic Theology at Ankara University (1954-1959), former Associate Professor of Arabic and Islamic Studies at the University of Bonn (1961-1966), and former Professor of Indo-Muslim Culture at Harvard University (1970-1992).

This eminent scholar of Oriental Religions, whom I have known for several years, has long been captivated by the work of that exemplar of Persian Sufism, Mawlānā Jalāl al-Dīn Rūmī. Her profound learning and scholarship is comparable to that of Hasan al-Baṣri. Yet her humility resembles that of Rābiʿa al-ʿAdawiya, the student of Hasan al-Baṣri. How rare it is to find two such attributes combined in one person, Annemarie Schimmel!

By publication of her English poetry in this volume Khaniqahi Nimatullahi Publications is honoured to present her with a humble token of our appreciation—by way of paying tribute to her lifetime's labour in Islamic Studies and Sufism.

Dr. Javad Nurbakhsh
London, August 1994

Variations on Maulana Jalaluddin Rumi's Thought

I Know

I know
There are no birch trees in Konya.
They grow farther north
under a silvery sky
mirrored in brownish brooks
in the Sarmathian steppe
or in upstate New York…

But I know
that Maulana said:
> Under the shade of your tresses
> so lovely and so cool
> my heart slept full of peace like
> the dust beneath a tree…

Dust out of which
grass will grow
to praise your mildness
heather will grow
to sing your beauty
(taking its hue from my blood-stainéd tears)
dust which one day
will be covered by gold
when you, dervish-birch,
will shed your leaves
to attain perfect peace,
poverty, purity, love.

Only your naked limbs stand there, on this silvery sky
and the wild grouse greet you
passing in winter nights into homelessness.

And I, the dust at your feet,
protect you, praying till spring…

Maulana Spoke

Maulana spoke:
    The lover
    weaves satin and brocade
    from tears, O friend, to spread it
    one day beneath your feet...
Only from tears, Maulana?
                    Every breath
Forms the weft of the endless fabric of love.

With every breath I weave the brocade of your name,
Golden letters inscribed in the satin-robe of my blood.
O, what garments have I prepared for you,
taking the ruddy dawn and the first green silk of spring,
star-embroidered velvet, and feather-light wool!
Every thought embellishes your name, O my friend,
Weaving into the fabric the turquoise domes of Iran,
Dyeing the yarn in the pearl-studded depth of the sea.

Every pulse beats the drum of primordial love
Every breath is the flute of impossible hope
Every goblet is filled with you

    And I weave
    ever new silken garments of words
                    only to hide you.

Without Your Speech

    "Without your speech the soul has no ear,
    Without your ear the soul has no tongue."

    Without your face, why need I my eyes?
    Without your eyes, I cover my face.
    Softer your touch than that of fresh snow,
    Diamond, cutting the stone of my heart.

4

Thirst

"Make thirsty me, O friend, give me no water!
Let me so love that sleep flees from my door!"
    Yes, sleep flees, if he sees the burning eyelids,
    He would be drowned if he would cross the sea
    Of tears; he would be poisoned
    If he should dare to drink
    That potent wine which you
    Poured in the goblet of my eyes:
    Those eyes which once beheld your radiant face
    And try to mirror it on every tear…
    …Those eyes which are a veil.

Make me more thirsty, friend, give me no water —
My thirst is proof that you are thirsty, too…

We Went Away

" We went away from your town
    and had not seen you enough,
We fell, alas, from your tree:
    fruits, unripe, deprived of your sap…
We went to the ruins and hoped
    to find a treasure like you;
Like serpents creeping in dust,
    that is how we went from your door…"
Reduced now to shadows, we passed
    from hopelessness and from hope.
The thorns turned to roses. No word.
    The desert was filled with black light.

Nimrod's Fire

Nimrod's fire became cool and pleasant.
All its flames and its sparks were luminous roses.
All the roses died with a smile, and their petals
Turned into rose-oil… O breeze full of fragrance!
One drop fell on me.

Now, in long nights my heart is one with the roses,
And towards dawn the roses turn into fire,
Burning away the thorns and the straw of my hopes,
Until I learn to die with a smile like the roses,
Until I am
    nothing but your fragrant oil…

Love? Do I Love?

Love? Do I love?
I do not know such words.

I close my eyes, and am your flute,
Long for your life-bestowing breath to teach me
to sing your praise.

I close my eyes, and am your harp,
reclining on your breast.
Your fingers which caress
My highstrung nerves make me able
to sing your praise.

I close my eyes, and am your lute.
I listen to your song, sometimes responding,
if you wish so.

With my eyes closed
I see you dancing with the whirling skies.
My heart: the drum.

Love? Do I love?
Take all the instruments,
throw them away and burn them, like wild rue,
The fire will lift up its hands in prayer,
The wind will carry off the selfless ashes
Into nowhere.

There I shall dance with you.

The Whole Night

The whole night I was weaving stuff of dreams,
of silken thoughts, of fragile threads of hope,
a spider web of much too lovely dreams,
a net to catch the first drops of the dew
and trap the sweet songs of the early birds
that swing at dawn so gently in the breeze.

The morning came.
Too heavy was the dew; some threads were torn;
the sun dried up whatever I had spun,
the cold wind of reality broke in
and there was nothing left...
no dream
        no hope
                no word.

There was another night,
another day
and still more spiderwebs
against the brassy sky
and other nets of letters in the brook
of hopelessness.

Now I am silent, and I weave no more.

> "When you don't speak, He will be on your lips.
> When you don't weave, the weaver will be He."

See, I Tried Everything

"See, I tried everything, went everywhere,
But never found a friend as dear as you;
I drank from all the fountains, tried the grapes,
But never tasted wine as sweet as you."

I read a hundred learned manuscripts:
In every letter I saw only you.
I washed away the letters with my tears;
A mirror was the shining page for you.

I heard your voice in every rustling breeze:
The snow, the grass were lovely veils for you;
I dived into the ocean without shore:
The lustrous pearls reflected only you.

Then came the storm;
The garden of my heart
Was shiv'ring in the cold, its leaves were shed.
There was the desert
And the barren cloud,
And silence. And
                the sun at midnight — you.

On the Road to Konya

REVERIE IN DECEMBER

Around the well
some purple sheep
the crescent moon
still half asleep

And the amethyst coloured road
points to nowhere

A lonely flute…
The camels dance
like passing clouds.
A star. A glance.

And my heart, in the winter wind
flies to nowhere.

HASAN DAGH

Never will you reach that silver mountain
which appears, like a cloud of joy,
in the evening light.

Never can you cross that lake of salt
which treacherously smiles at you
in the morning mist.

Every step on this road takes you farther away
from home, from flowers, from spring.
Sometimes the shade of a cloud will dance on the way
Sometimes you rest in a ruined caravanserai
seeking the truth from the blackish tresses of smoke
Sometimes you walk a few steps
with a kindred soul
                    only to lose him again.

You go, and go
torn by the wind, burnt by the sun,
and the shepherd's flute
tells you "the Path in Blood"

until you cry no more

until the lake of salt
is only your dried-up tears
        which mirror the mountain of joy
        that is closer to you than your heart.

Letters to
Nowhere

Song

You are, dear, a birch
beyond time and space.
I can't be the soil
to nourish your heart.
I have to be wind
to caress your hair.

Remember

Remember?
There were some unicorns
in the forest of yore.
Playful and white
they walked through the waning moon
in early dawn.
Lilies grew out of their steps.

But, dear, once you smiled at them
and they bowed at your feet,
melting like dew,
And I
cried
envying them.

You Were a Blue Star

You were a blue star.
Then, you were a red bird
on a snow-covered tree.
Melting, the bird was a pearl,
unfolding into a rose.

Again, you were wine,
and after a while
a lonely flute.

Every moment you change your form.
But under every guise
my heart recognizes your heart,
and the ear of my soul
hears your eternal word
in every sound
even
when you break the glass.

Journey

Through dawns, through clouds, beyond stars
I have to go and to go
to find the flower of alchemy
in the garden of souls.

If I could find it,
opening its petals like crimson wounds...

If I should find it
my heart would open like crimson wounds
and I would begin
once more the way through the gamut of elements,
and I would be
dust at your feet
wind in your hair
water in your eyes
sunlight, to add to your smile.

Then, all consumed,
I would be just a kiss
to talk with you with no words.

I Write to You

I write to you
but fire
leaps out of the stone of my heart
and destroys the paper.

I write to you
but water
wells up from the rocks of my eyes
and dissolves the paper.

Should I, then, write
with the red lines of my tears
on my parchment cheeks?
Or rather
give the grey ashes into the wind's hands
to carry them to your porch?

After a while
    maybe
you will hear my voice
in the dried-up leaves
in autumnal dusk
    Maybe
you will read my words
on a peacock's tail
sparkling on summer lawns.
They are always there:
in the poppies' sleep
in a toad's golden eyes
in a kitten's fur.
    Why do we need words
    to tell the endless tale
    of Beauty and Love?

The Painter's Letter

I love you.
Your eyebrows
are the prayer niche to which I have turned;
Your tresses are hyacinths near a rose parterre.

I saw you only once, O sun of my days,
and tried to preserve that moment of grace
in every line of my work:
Every red means your mouth,
every white your longed-for breast,
every black is your mole…

And when Doomsday comes
I shall carry this portrait with me:
        "Look, Lord! — this is all I have done!"

Oh, Could We but Embrace You

Oh, could we but embrace you:
we: shore, and you the sea,
or dwell amidst your blossoms:
we: birds, and you the tree.

But we are prints on water
and traces in the sand;
Like snowflakes or stray feathers
we are in no one's hand.

Forever separated
from our home and root —
Oh, if your breath would touch us,
we'd love to be your flute…

19

Zulaykha's First Letter to Yusuf

I wait for the moon
to rise on the eastern sky —
        perhaps you have looked at her
that I mirror her
in the lake of my tears
in the sea of my dreams.

Reflected in thousands of drops
your smile sinks deep into the oyster of recollection
— pearl of all pearls —

Zulaykha's Second Letter to Yusuf

I use the choicest papyri
when I write to you.
I draw my letters
with hammered gold
        and lapis lazuli.
Only my name is written with ashes,
for your glory has burnt my heart and my name,
for you have consumed all my thought.

When you enter, it's day
        even at dusk
when you smile
the orchard opens in bloom
        even in fall.
When you go
it is desert-night
        even in spring.

I can call you only by words
which blossom out of your name,
I can offer you only those gems
which always belonged to you,
    but they are covered, my friend,
        with the ashes
            of my lost name.

Zulaykha's Third Letter to Yusuf

I called the best painters
from all over the world
to decorate my house.
They looked at you, and each of them tried
to interpret your beauty
in color, marble, or tiles:

    Rosegardens and fruits,
    the sun in his golden boat,
    white herons among the nymphacas,
    black carnations, and turquoise waves...
All the pictures were only a faint reflection
as if my broken lute were to echo, dimly,
the primordial song of love.

Once more I called the best artists
from all over the world
to decorate my house.
They looked at you, and each of them brought
A mirror to reflect your face.
    Thousands of mirrors — steel, diamond, glass —
    each one reflecting the other's light
        — light, borrowed from you —
and each of them was a veil.

Year after year
I looked at the paintings
I gazed at the mirrors
until the djinns of despair
trailed their grey trains
through the vast desert, along the hills,
and my palace was filled with sand.

I closed my eyes,
tired since long, dried-up, weary eyes.
No picture, no mirror, no word.

Now
every drop of my blood
is an eye
to contemplate you
without a veil.

Yusuf's Letter to Zulaykha

Please — don't write any more!
Every day
you shower sweet words upon me, like dates,
you fill my house with the fragrance of your musk-black ink,
and you spread your tresses under my feet.

I know
you are more radiant than the sun,
more beautiful than the moon,
and I love you.
But I am afraid of you.
Your smiling eyes burn my heart,
your tears poison me.

Believe me:
I am not chaste,
I am not virtuous and pure,
I am just afraid…

I control my lord's fields
stalk by stalk.
I measure the harvest
grain by grain,
and at night my fingers play
with the rosary of the sky
counting star by star
in perfect serenity.

But the torrent of your love
destroys my account,
tears apart my luminous beads,
and spoils my neatly plaited white gown…
How disquieting…!

Please, don't write any more!

Khidr's Complaint

You envy me.
But can you imagine
what it means, not to die?
Can you imagine, O men,
how terrifying the valley was, and how dark
where I tasted the bitter Water of Life
unwillingly,
unwittingly?

You envy me.
But I roam, with parched lips and wet eyes
day after day, year after year
in the purple shades of thirsty deserts,
in the turquoise waves of pulsating seas
seeking
behind shifting dunes the origin of the sand,
behind restless waves the origin of the sea.

Unending quest.

Sometimes
I find a garden, a meadow, a tree:
Rose-faces, narcissus-eyes, jasmine-breasts,
and I forget my pain
as long as a swallow's flight.
But the jasmine withers,
the narcissus fades,
and the rose petals drop like blood.

Then, I return
to the blackish letters and ancient scripts on yellow papyri,
to the magic signs engraved in stone and in glass
to forget the temptation
        and to break the spell once and for all.
But the zodiac bars
the gate of liberation

And time
has transformed my tears into pearls,
into rubies my blood.

I give them to you, O men,
I give you the wreath of pearls and the rings,
 the ruby bezels, the crowns,
 my miracles and
       my immortality.

I give them to you
for that one hour
when He, heart of my heart
unveils His face before me,
when His rose-fire consumes my life in one kiss,
and my weary soul closes its wings in peace.

Farhad's Letter to Shirin

Sometimes
I create a beautiful bird,
feeding him with my sweet dreams
and the water of tears
until his wings
grow strong, and he brings
you into that garden which I have planted for you
under the snow.

Its roses, its fragrant jasmine
vaguely reflect your cheeks and your smile.
Its brooklet, its fountains, its dew
spring from the eyes of your longing friend;
its cooling breeze
is the lover's sigh.

Surrounded by moth-like doves
    (ashes of all burnt hearts)
the cypresses wait;
candles, formed
from the black light of bewilderment.
There, we walk without words,
and I engrave your face
in the emerald rock
beyond the skies.

Shirin's Letter to Farhad

You dream of a garden
which you water with rivers of sweetest milk,
and of my face
engraved in the emerald plate
far beyond the skies.

If you claim to be a true lover
make your every vein a river through which
your blood rushes toward not-being.
nourishing only tulips,
    the shrouds of the martyrs of love.
Make your every nerve a road
to travel to annihilation,
and dig up the rock of existence
until you find
the treasure of love,
    the radiant rubies of poverty.

Consumed by their fire, my friend,
you will be mine.

Layla's Letter to Majnun

You don't ask the birds any more
to tell you news about me.
You gave them
your heart to dwell,
your hair to nest.

They have carried away my heart,
and the glaring sun at the high noon of despair
dries up my eyes' wells

But yonder gazelles
that drink from your salty tears
become immortal.

Majnun's Letter to Layla

I love you so much —
But you are a scent
that fades away
when the night is spent..

I love you so much —
but you are a song
on everyone's lips —
and the nights are long.

I love you so much —
but you are a dune,
ever new shifting sand
ever new changing moon…

And I count the stars
And I am that tune,
And I am the scent,
and the silvery dune…

A Plane Tree

A plane tree
stretched out its hand
to touch your hair

A white bird
sailed, full of peace,
in your heart's air

A cloud's shade
stretched out its hand,
led you away
        into Nowhere.

New England

This is no Country

This is no country where the stork repeats
his pious call "Thine is the kingdom, Lord!"
and not a garden where the nightingale
pours out his heart in longing for the Rose.
I never heard the dove ask: "Where, oh where?"
Nor did the plane-tree lift its hands in prayer;
The violets that grow along the street
are trampled down; they do not meditate.

But yesterday
at noon
over the dirty snow
        over the blackish roofs
two seagulls sailed across the icy blue
whiter than snow, two lilies of the sky

And their crystal-like wings
reflected the sun
        Light upon light…

The weary bird of my soul
joined, full of awe,
their silent hymn.

Raga Pahari

– I –

I've never been to the hills,
but I know
there's a crystalline lake
blue as a peacock's neck,
as the kingfisher's wing.

While rain is drizzling all night
       slowly turning to snow
while wind is raging all night
       scourging the dismal clouds
    there are almond trees, there are does
    dancing like dew drops at dawn

       and the Beloved… he comes
       scattering rubies and pearls
       sweeter than death…

The ice of my heart
dissolves into tears
to water the orchard of dreams,
the bitter almonds of dreams…

– II –

All my blue peacocks ate
the bitter almonds of dreams
All my kingfishers drank
the salty water of tears.
All my birds are now dead.

I wander alone
    without dreams,
    without tears
in an alley of shadowless trees
along a motionless stream

Only the beats of my heart
    irregular little beats
tell me that I'm still alive.

– III –

A new bird tries
to sing the verse which the wind
writes on the river's page
and a young daring twig
begins to dance, and its shade
creates strange patterns of hope
on the marbleized grey sky.

    Then,
a shiv'ring cloud's tears
wash the picture away...

Will the twig dance again?
Will the rays of the sun
write a still sweeter verse?

Reflections

The cat plays
with the reflections on the wall
of reflections on a knife's blade
of a swinging lamp.

The pond smiles.
Its ripples reflect
a silvery cloud's hem
that mirrors the sun.

My heart
caught in the fists of despair
waits
for a sign of the light.

A reflection's reflex
would be enough.

In Memory of Tufan

"April is the cruelest month,"
Its untimely snow
buries the hopeful buds,
covers the trusting twigs.
April gives, and it takes:
Gives us the radiant joy,
carries away what we love,
mothers, brothers. and friends.
Why then lament a cat's death?

We loved, oh, we loved his soft gait,
his purring, his eyes, and his sleep
"Love, and be it a cat,"
Thus spoke the Prophet, and we
loved him, the silent black friend,
soft-pawed and wise,
who knew how to lick
        our tears of despair.

Dear little friend — lift your paws,
pray for us here in this world,
pray for all those who still love,
all those whose tears
fall on a grave
as the magnolia buds
open and gently dissolve.

Dreaming in December of Shalimar

A soft-winged dove
on a cypress tree
in the silvery moon
    I thought of your hands

A cypress tree
and a soft-winged dove
in the silvery moon
    I thought of your gait

A silvery moon
o'er a cypress tree
surrounded by doves
    I thought of your face

    How peacefully slept
the dove in her nest
on the cypress tree
close to the brook of my tears,
close to the fountain of life
which reflects the face of the moon!

But tonight…
a freezing raven
perches on a bleak birch,
and the Muharram moon's scimitar
slaughters a helpless heart.

Every Broken Hope

Every broken hope,
every shattered dream
strips off a bit of your skin.
Slowly, you are flayed alive
    most gently.

Forget the salt they rub into your flesh
    most gently.

For the glory of love
and the glory of God
will all be there
in your bleeding limbs
which reveal the light of the soul
    if you are patient enough.

There is No Love

There is no love
but for the First Beloved.
You tell us different names,
but it is He whom you mean.

Friends, lovers, and guests —
they all talked to you,
taught you to suffer, to grow,
slowly to understand the language if not of birds,
of naked trees shivering in the storm…
and each of them was but a spark
of a fire that flared up high
on touching your soul
to burn you time after time,
        poor, blesséd moth!

There is no love
but for the First Friend
whose naked glory you hide
under hundreds of veils.

The Silver Bull in the Metropolitan Museum

Millions of years of silent sufferings
of beasts, of trees, of stones and of stars
were poured into the offering bowl
which the silver bull
lifts up to the gods with an immortal smile,
grateful in servitude.

Indian Summer

The Rajah of Kotah
entertains his birds,
teaching them strange songs of love,
and his elephants dance
on the eyes of white deer.
Trees turn to gold,
turn to copper, and flames; and the songs
of childhood resound
while our hands do not meet,
while the Celestial Pen
writes mysterious words
with the blue of the sky,
with the gold of the leaves, and the salmon's pink:
words to be read
by the birds and the deer,
sung by the elephants, and
        never to be divulged.

At the End of the ACLS Lectures, 1980

The purple archangel's wing,
the archangel's iron wing
creates a colorful play:
    Soft silvery mist at sweet dawn,
    A dying deer in the dust,
    Museums, students, some cats…
They come and they go and they come
On the magic conveyer belt.

I take them and put them away,
waiting for more to appear:
    Wild fragrance of lilacs,
    Wind over the plains,
    Green rocks, and the sparks
    Of tulips, and rains…
They go and they come and they go
On the magic conveyer belt.

I take them no longer away;
I wait for the end of the day,

I wait for the silent night
when the archangel's purple wing
will cover the eyes of my heart
and there will be nothing but You.

INDIA!

September 1985 in New York

Manhattan dissolves into clouds of despair.
Oppressive heat,
and no sleep at night.

With wide-open eyes
I find myself in the velvet tent:
    velvet, red like the wine
    which we sip from bowls of white jade
    and opium dreams
    rising from emerald cups,
    carry us further away.

The cosmic dance
of gold and green leaves
whirls through the Central Park, stops,
and is resumed again. Buses and cars,
turning in maddening whorls,
spinning like feathers on headhunters' masks,
suddenly freeze into flowers of silk…

Wondrous birds open their wings,
and the lion devours
his prey with passionless charm.
Elephants rush through the walls of my heart,
and cheetahs tiptoe on shimmering rugs.
Weapons open like buds,
and never-shed blood
has turned into rubies
on dagger hilts.

Perspicacious eyes
look through the centuries, and
sensuous lips
still sing of love and despair.
Poets are weighed against gold.

But who could tell
how the fingers looked
that have woven these moonbeam-like silks
and transformed the hard stone into twigs,
     into flowers that swing in the breeze
         when the plaintive goat bleats near the village well
     just before dawn?
Which saint keeps their names
and utters blessings for them?

I walk through their smiles and their tears,
through the perfect beauty of things,
breathless with gratitude.
And Manhattan dissolves
into golden mist
on the other side of the moon...
     farther away, oh, my heart
     than the silent sigh
     of a jade terrapin...

Journeys

In Flight

Carried away by the falcon Love,
The heart finds itself
    on the glaciers of joy.
Superbly happy,
It gazes into the sun;
Superbly lonely
It craves for a cloud's flighty shade
Before it dissolves in the light;
Before it is shattered again
In the dark of despair
Where Your hand will gather its shards.

Autumnal Ghazni

Centuries old is the wind.
The mountains gaze, empty-eyed.
From crumbling ruins and tombs
grow delicate flowers of stone.
A fragment of verse on a wall.

The plane trees stretch out their hands—
hands filled with gold,
ready to shed their wealth…
True dervishes, souls without greed.

Our feet touch the dust
of the tombs of saints,
of scholars, of kings,
dust, softer than silk,
warm from the embers that sometimes flare up
in candles of longing and love
      (poplars, surrounding the town,
      which reflect the glory of yore…)
Prayers resound in the wings of ash-coloured doves.

Now, the wind sings
in the Garden of Truth,
and the mountains remember
the days of love.

Marib

The gardens of Marib
are covered with sand,
but Sheba's sweet smile
still colours the land.
      Enchanted enchantress —
      annihilating herself in Love
      she vanquishes death with a smile.

48

Prague 1978

ABSURD AUTUMNAL SONG

A king's skull
looks at a world that once was his own —
Around non-existent lips
a smile, half amused and half sad,
like the City of Gold
in the non-light
of an eclipsed moon;
like the diamond dust
on temples, dark blue
in a jungle of hands.

And the child-saint dreams
in the cool, brisk breeze
that smashes the goblet of hope
    that fans the embers of hope.

The bittersweet scent of purple carnations —
    you still think of it?

Some yellow flowers
in modest backyards
and orange bindweed
at the hip of low-shouldered huts —
tiny reflections of suns
that once caressed golden domes.

We glean the leftovers of dreams,
and the few grains of smile
are sweeter, I think,
than the kisses of yore.

Saiful Muluk Lake in Kaghan

The fairy Badi'ul-jamal sings:

But these mountains were part of my heart!

I knew them when I was young
for they were the land
where I once cried for my friend
who saw me there in his dream
     after bowing his head
     in a magic bowl
which showed him the Real World —
a world made of radiant light,
a world where the body is soul
and where his beloved waits
     to teach him a sweeter embrace...

I was that beloved, and I
fell back into Time, into Space
because I waited for him
because I loved him too much...

And now, I see yonder hills,
those hills, born of my heart,
those brooks, born of my tears,
mirrors of worlds that once were my own...
and my broken wings touch the dust —
     your dust, O my love.

Wales

The emerald meadows
are studded with pearls.

> The emerald softens to grass
> and the pearls dissolve into buds,
> each blooming into a lamb

Near a river, icy and swift,
an aged oak tree bends down;
the river kisses its eyes
and the trout builds a nest in its hair.

Old chapels resound
with the litany of the flute
with the shepherd's tunes
> which he sang for his flower-sheep
> which he sings for my heart to sleep.

The vaults of the ruined church
write illegible words
in the patient dust —
> only the flower-sheep
> can read these mysterious signs
>> which transform them into soft clouds
>> reflected on emerald lawns
>> and mirrored in crystalline brooks
until the night's scented cloak
> covers the world.

Only the fragrance remains
> of a lonely bird's song
and the pearls and the clouds and the sheep
> are all one
>> in the deep vale of sleep...

Sunset in Anatolia

Long rows of grey camels
walk slowly over the sky
led by the sun's golden rope
toward the west.
They carry heavy loads of pearls of rain,
gossamer sashes of silvery haze,
black velvet embroidered with purple and gold.

Sometimes the wind caresses their feather-light wool,
tells them of meadows, of brooklets, far, far away.

One of the camels kneels and kisses a yellow rose,
dies at her feet,
dissolved in tears.

But the caravan moves
slowly
led by the sun's crimson rope
into Nowhere.

The Great Mughals

Babur in Delhi (1526)

I craved for fame
and I left my home.
I crossed seven rivers
and seven ranges of hills.

The plains opened their arms
like a bride, ageless and bright,
to embrace me, gently and warm,
to nourish my hungry soul
with the choicest fruits, and with wine.

Sometimes,
the blood of my soldiers coloured the soil
        — the meadows, lush paradise —
Sometimes
fortresses rose, red like flames.
And there were more rivers, more tears.

Now you think that I am at peace.
Still clouds and the scorching sun
bring visions… victories, pearls,
glory, immortal, and joy.

But my heart
lies buried on yonder hill
where modest flowers grow between stones
under the azure sky,
where an icy wind
wakes up the mountains at dawn…

It would be good to come home.

Fatehpur Sikri

Akbar speaks:

Thousands of days and nights
passed over my heart — a rock
on which peacocks nested, and hawks.
Then, the stonecutter's axe
touched my heart,
and torrents of blood
colored the rock.

I dug from the quarry, my heart,
most beautiful stones, to erect
a doorway toward the Lord —
  higher than my pride
  deeper than my love
  broader then my mind
And the stonecutter's eye
polished the stones by its glance,
and the sound of his voice
set them aright.

But men saw only the strength
of walls and palace and dome —
They took the symbol for truth.

And I left the stones to themselves.

Sometimes I come back
where the fragrant grass
decks out an old path,
and the gentle breeze
touches my hand
in autumnal love.

  I know:
  the walls of my heart
  enshrine that white pearl
  which can never be found.

Gwalior

Muhammad Ghauth Gwaliori speaks:

I walked through the skies.
I wove the stars and the moon
    in harmonious patterns, each one
a symbol of one Name Divine.

Majesty is the star that reveals itself here,
overlooking the hills:
In the naked crude idols that watch
    the steep path, and the caves,
in the pillars of lion-man shape,
in the dark blue tiles of the wall.
    I read the letters that will be sent out
        from the prison's heart
    I hear poets' and rulers' laments
        from the prison's heat —
Grandeur, revealed in reflections of Hell.

And yet
the autumnal breeze
carries the fragrance of grass,
    of clover and honey, of love.

I walked through the skies.
The five jewels of wisdom were mine
    in constellations
    in meditations
    in signs.
I read the stars like a book
    The Milky Way was my scarf,
    the zodiac my rosary.
The harmony of the spheres
resounded in Tansen's sitar.

I walked through the skies.
      the scent of clover and grass
      the touch of marble and clouds
      the sight of idols and rocks
      the sound of music and death
      the taste of honey and smoke
were parts of the star of life.

But I know more than life.

I have reached the black light
      beyond the green stars
I have found the Great Name
      beyond all these names.

Now, the spider Time
weaves an intricate marble net
over my tomb —
      stars that point to Nowhere.

Epitaphs for Three Mughal Ladies

NURJAHAN

I was Jahangir's most beloved wife,
Light of his world, and pivot of his life.
He ruled the country, and I ruled his heart.

Yet, I remained a stranger. No one comes
to lit a candle on my tomb so that
a moth may burn its wings.
At sunset sings
no bird for me, and lonely are the nights.

For the nightingales dwell
near Jahangir's rose-coloured tomb.

MUMTAZ MAHAL

I was the ruler's most beloved wife,
Joy of his nights, and fragrance of his life.
But I melted like dew in the rising day.

From the rock of his pain,
the black marble of grief
grew a pearl-white jasmine
at the river bank of his tears.

Now, both of us sleep
under the dome of jasmine.

NADIRA BEGUM

I was my prince's most beloved wife,
A shining gem, a mirror for his life.

They chased him, and
I followed him
through desert paths —
　　only to die in his arms.

His last few soldiers carried me home
That I might sleep at the feet of the Saint,
that I might rest under roses in peace.
But he, oh! was slain!

Would that he be buried near me
that I kiss his bloodstained mouth,
that I cover his wounds with my hair!

Why had he to die for his love?
Why was he killed for a dream?

Khankhanan's Mausoleum

"To praise you is as if the mango tree
sheds golden fruits into the gardener's lap:
    'It's you that tended us!'"...

Thus spoke your poet. Then, the twilight fell;
the gardens which you planted lie now waste,
your library turned into dried-up trees
whose colored leaves were carried far away
by cruel winds.
           And naked stands your tomb.

And yet — at dawn some dervish (or some lonely bird?)
    still sings your praise —

Aurangzeb's Last Portrait

Bent over his prayer beads,
Which Name Divine does he invoke?
    O Overpowering
                O Everlasting
    O Lord...

Weary fingers cling to the string,
counting the beads, sigh by sigh.
    O Overpowering
                O All-Subduing
    O Lord...

Bead by bead drops from his hand,
red, like his brothers' blood.
    O Overpowering
                O Death-bestowing
    O Lord...

Tear by tear falls like the beads —
Which Name Divine does he invoke?
    O Overpowering
                O All-Forgiving
    O Lord...

Sufi Shrines

Uchh Sharif

The dust
of numberless crumbled prayers
covers the ground.

But the blue of the sky,
    the light of radiant faith
crystallized in the tiles
shows you that grace
    is greater than guilt
tells you that hope
    is stronger than death

and that the pattern of life
    is always perfect.
        Don't cry.

Somewhere near Multan

All roads come from Eternity.

The bullock carts, and the goats,
sad little donkeys with hanging ears
in the fields, near the thatched huts;
camels, carrying cotton bales, day after day.

From the colourful trucks
blossom the dreams of the poor,
and the reed longs to sing of man's fate.

The nameless heroines of poverty,
lifting their pitchers, await
the water of life.

All roads point to Eternity.

And their centre rests
under the sky-like dome
in the heart of the saint.

Dewa Sharif

To be sure — the stone floor of dervish cells
is a hard bed.

But the immaculate song
of the old dervish
filled this night, too, with fragrance and peace,
and the light green dome
was the same at dusk and at dawn,
undisturbed by the world.

Rudauli Sharif

A tree
stretches out his arm
    over the sleeping saint.

Everywhere the word Truth
    Truth, Truth, and Truth
resounds from the leaves, from the mud.

Inside the crumbling wall
grows a lonely rose.

Kichhauchha Sharif

Rain drizzles
night after night.
Rain pours
day after day.
Green like a corpse the lukewarm pond
that surrounds the castle of djinns.

A toad-man leads us through mud,
a vulture perches on a bone —
        a minaret's finger-bone —
The rhythmic beat of mad heads
on the walls, on the floor,
the screaming of evil djinns
through the mouth of women. The hair
disheveled; dismembered, near-dead
they scratch our mind with their nails.

And the toad-man with greedy eyes
squats on the stair,
eager to eat our hearts…

Qasur – Bullhe Shah's Tomb

"Our greatest poet" – they say –
"Pride of the Punjab" he is called,
immortal and sweet are his songs,
repeated time and again
on TV, in ev'ryday talk.

But his tomb is the dead heart
of a fading town of the past.
There live some faqirs, to be sure.

Between two hemp-drunken dreams
    (dreams of a Paradise, green,
    with rivers of honey and milk,
    a garden that's Love, only Love
    and everything is The Friend)
between two hemp-drunken dreams
they stumble toward the shrine,
clasping with fleshless hands
the veil that covers the tomb,
craving for shelter and love,
pressing their foreheads in dust —

for the mute and deaf dust,
    touched by the feet of the saint
shows greater compassion than those
who claim to admire the saint…

Evening in Tajpur

"Mansoor, oh Mansoor
His head caressed the gallow's tree
Mansoor, Mansoor
His bridal bed – the gallow's tree —
Mansoor —
Quenching his thirst
with the wine of pain
beating the drum
he danced in his chain —
Mansoor, oh Mansoor..."

Hundreds of years have passed
since he wandered through Sind;
hundreds of years...
burning wind,
and a river of tears.

Out of his steps
blossomed jasmine-white shrines
which carry the fragrance of love
as do the fields of sweet peas.

Tonight, the fireflies dance.
The evening breeze,
sweet,
leads our steps
to the rose-bed, the tree
where all our dreams end

"...quenching his thirst
with eternal wine,
submersed in love,
without Mine and Thine —
Mansoor...
Mansoor..."

Impressions from

India

Khuldabad

A dervish
stretched out his hand
with his beggar's bowl.
    But the bowl
    was a bleeding heart.

Bombay

The magic pen
forms snowflakes, flowers, and stars,
mandalas, beautiful forms,
whose axis is loneliness.

An unfeeling sky
hangs over the leaden bay.
People walk, noisy and dumb,
puppets of paper-maché.
Noise, grating my heart,
and no balm of a smile…
Shiva has closed all his eyes,
receding into Himself.

Poona: Parvati's Shrine

A caterpillar —
little black line in a silver fur —
moves ever so gently
over the stones
at the goddess's feet.
Dancing, it seems,
to the music, he knows
of his future flights.

Bidar: Mahmud Gawan's tomb.

These too are dreams, dreams like the broken tiles
that once adorned a prince's spacious halls
and still resound with laughter of his friends...
dreams, dark as tulips in their bloodstained shrouds
and smiling like the roses when they die.

Tonight, the stars watch o'er the lonely tomb.

Soon, the new morning comes, and then we'll know
the patterns of the tulips and the tiles;
the meaning of a rose, which, dying, smiles.

Bijapur

IBRAHIM RAUZA

Out of the whirling dust
that turns into children, chickens, and goats,
grows a tulip garden of stone.
At the end of a grimy road
the most serene of all tombs
— too beautiful to be true —
a golden jewelry box
in the afternoon light.

GANJ UL -'ILM'S SHRINE.

Four baby owls
in the morning mist
at an old saint's tomb.
They earnestly watch
the stranger who looks
for the Treasure of Wisdom that rests
under the crumbling walls.
    And a feather's soft kiss
    touches the seeker's hair.

Golconda - Hyderabad

Dreams
float in the dusk —
too many dreams:
of love, of beauty, of death...
And never shed tears, crystallize
into cornelian seals,
engraved with His name.

CHAR MINAR

Once, a king
dreamt of his true love
    on the other side of the river.
All his tears
became lustrous pearls
    on the other side of the river.
So he built
a diamond locket for them
    on the other side of the river,
and her smile
turned into rubies,
    into silver, the waves of the river...

The fragrance of love
still fills yonder lanes
    on the other side of the river...

FALAKNUMA

To Mujeeb Yar Jung

Once
its roof touched the skies,
and the ladies looked
over the smiling town,
over the rolling hills.

Once
its gardens were paradise,
and the ladies walked
over fragrant lawns,
over marble stairs.

Now
the palace has closed its eyes.
The city forgot its smile,
and frustrated fog
clings to the hills.

Only our steps resound
in the wide, dark rooms —
rooms which enshrine
pearl-studded dreams…

FEAST AT PURANI HAVELI

The haunted palace
resounds with songs.
The doves dance
around the lamps,
and the owls, amazed, shake their heads.

Far, far away
the noise of the teeming streets:
stars, falling in ponds,
and the rhythms of drums.

Out of a broken heart
grows the slender date-palm of grief,
shedding its fruits
on the meadows of joy —
fruits, sweeter than death.

Kashmir

DUSK IN SRINAGAR.

Sadness covers the lake
— soft layers of haze —
The plane leaves that burned
in ruby fires have turned
into ashes.
       The hills
resound with silence, and tears
flow from the eyes of Neshat.

GULMARG - BABA RISHI

He took the mountains as coat,
as turban, the sky.
Eagles and yaks kissed his feet
and the kindly cloud brought him milk.
The saint's radiant smile
made the meadows bloom, and it filled
with fragrance the Deodar trees.
    But he did not see them.
    He stared
    only
    at God.
And his tears
grew into brooks, into lakes,
into a stream that flows
down to the lost land of Love.

Fayzabad

"The bazaar of Fayzabad
was a garden full of fruits
    fruits and silk for ladies fair.
The bazaar of Fayzabad
was a garden full of flowers,
golden coins and silver coins,
heaped on trays, narcissus-like
    bangles for the ladies fair..."

Well said, old Mir Hasan, but —
The bazaar of Fayzabad
is a shadow of a tale...
No silver coins left,
no flower-like gold...

Only a hungry young cow
eats golden banana peel
from a girl's silver hand...

Rajasthan: Kuchaman

God is the primordial fort.
    We graze in the lowlands
    Like camels and cows,
    enjoying His shade
        and the sudden blue
        of a peacock's neck.

But day after day
    a convoy of souls
    climbs up the steep path
    to conquer the fortress
    and its treasures of joy.
    Slipp'ry the stones — and at every step
    new horizons unfold
    to confuse their eyes and their dreams.
    Thorns tear asunder their skirts;
    the arrows of fate pierce their limbs;
    the elephants of despair
    trample many to death.

    Some learn from the kites
    to circle like songs in the air,
    their wings reflecting the sun.

    And some even enter the gate.
    But subtler snares catch their minds:
    The pond full of Water of Life;
    pavilions with heavenly songs
    and rooms, decked with mirrors of gold.
        O sweetest fatigue!

    But those who have reached
    the secret of Love,
    they enter the flames
    that consume fear and hope.

Songs from Sind

Marui in Omarkot

I love you.
There were deserts between us.
But now, the desert is green.
The rain of grace fell
and we eat
berries and fruits of the land.

I love you.
I waited for you,
I prayed for you
until the walls of Omarkot fell
and the desert was mine again.
The silver moon
kisses your feet,
and young camels dance in the sand.

I love you.
The desert blooms,
and we quench our thirst —
O my love — our thirst...

Sassi in the Desert

I walk
and the blood of my feet
    transforms the stones into roses.

I walk
and the tears of my eyes
    water the desert shrubs,
Every day the same sun,
    scorching, merciless, white,
And at nightfall the wind, cutting my heart and my hope.

I walk out of myself
And the desert is you.
The paths are throbbing like veins,
and tenderly touches my hand
your skin, soft as sand.

I wander through you,
drinking the salty water that flows from your eyes,
sleeping at night in your arms
when you cover my weary limbs
with your garment of stars.
    And I am
one with the beats of your heart,
one with your breath, with the wind.

Sassi Abri

Once I longed for your kiss.
    But kisses are flighty like bees.
Once I longed for your hand.
    But hands touch only the skin.

Now I have passed through the hills,
the rocks where blue serpents sing
a tune that burns skin and bones.

I envy my eyes
which have seen you once:
tearing them out,
I feed the crows.

And each of my limbs
Beholds you now without veil.

Heer Ranjha

O sisters! Sisters! I'm ill!
A snake has bitten my foot!

> O sister, sister! No snake
> has bitten you in the fields!
> Was not the reedflute a snake
> that stealthily poisoned your soul?

O sisters! Sisters! The sound
of the flute has pierced my heart
and only the one who has played
the flute — he can help me survive!

> We'll bring the flute player near —
> His flute will cure you, my dear!

Listening to his tunes
Heer's heart was healed.
Listening to his tunes
She felt that all worldly concerns
> were falling from her like dead leaves,
> that Ranjha was only a sign
> of the Real Beloved.
Looking at him she remembered, nay, knew
> that she lived through his breath,
> that she was nothing
>> but a song of his flute.

Adam Durkhana

The walls of the fortress of Law
are stronger than stones.
No way for escape.
The walls of the fortress of Law
enshrine a young heart
    that dreams of a rose.

Who played the lute, say? Who sang
of beauty, of longing, of power, of death?
Petal by petal
    a heart's bud opened.

But the fortress of Law
has a sevenfold wall.

Wrestling with fate
    he opened the gate —
        and the petals fell on his hand.

He who played the lute,
he who sang
poured out his heart, nightingale-like.
The steep rock was daubed with his blood
    and the rose died with a smile...

A brooklet gushed forth from their tears,
and the fragrance of Deodar trees
    preserves their last sighs...

Sur Sorathi

He rode
on a dappled horse
a hawk on his hand
through the rugged rocks.
    He dreamt
    of the evening breeze,
    for Sorathi's eyes
    were a sapphire lake.
        He heard
        far away a song
        as bitter as life
        and as sweet as death.

The evening breeze turned to storm,
to fire the sapphire lake.
And Saturn, triumphant, saw
the king's severed head

But the song still resounds —
    a farewell to fire and wind,
    a farewell to water and earth,
    a farewell to life
                and to pain.

– II –

The peacocks screamed,
trembling in unfulfilled lust.

The angel was waiting for him,
and stretched out his hand.
The king saw the black pearl.
Obeying the order of Love
he bowed his head.

The angel opened his wings,
and darkness covered the world.
Lightnings sprang from his heart
and set Girnar aflame.

But the tears that fell from his eyes
made the meadows bloom
and the peacocks dance.

Sur Sohni

- I -

I was never afraid
of crossing the waves;
I know the current, the ford,
and even the sharks were my friends.

But today I am tired.
Why have I always to swim
that he may enjoy sweetest fruits?
Why does he not come to seek me,
leaving his island behind,
leaving his star-eyed cows?

Hopelessness batters my heart —
Will it shatter my jar?

- II -

I dreamt of a road
that led to the sea.
I slept without you
near a shadowless tree.

I carried a jar,
a jar full of pain.
I needed your hand,
but I called you in vain.

So, my vessel broke...
And I...
        I was drowned...

– III –

You think of the time before Time
when your heart was bound to your Lord.
You remember the day
when two drops from the sea —
    the primordial ocean of God —
were cast on the shore of this world,
    separated by Time.

You remembered the ocean's depth
and you longed for that drop,
a sign from the sea,
    night after night.

You took as life buoy the jar
    that was filled with His Name
    to carry you safely along
to the shore where the cows' star-like eyes
served you as beacon lights.
    And every night
    the faithful jar with His Name
    carried you back to the house
where they loathed you, 'Adulteress, accursed!'

But tonight
your vessel will break
and you'll reach the abyss of Love
the fiery ocean of Love
    where all names are burnt
    where all signs are lost...

Sur Momal Rano

My gown like a rose,
My shawl like a leaf —
They say that my smile
Dispells a man's grief.

I eat and I walk,
I drink and I talk
with all those who think
that the tears on my robe
      are genuine pearls.

But behind my eyes
stretches the endless garden of dreams.
There, I walk in the autumnal haze
until I reach
the shore of the sea,
of the burning ocean of Love.
Breathless with adoration —
I sink into its depths…

Crystalline, light upon light,
Moon, more than moon -
      His Face…

And I return to my friends,
My hands full with jetsam of words…
Mute, with no tongue
to tell what I've seen
                  without eyes.

Sur Lila Chanesar

The walls echoed your laughter,
and the flowers reflected your smile.
You slept
on colourful quilts
in your husband's arms.

But you wanted the stars.
You took them, a diamond string
to play with them as with beads,
and forsook your love for a toy.

> The moon veiled her face,
> and the dawn blushed from shame.

And now —
the rocks echo your sighs,
and the dried-up ponds stare at you.

You sleep
on an ashen bed
where the lepers lie.

But you possess your tears,
more precious than diamond strings.

They'll adorn you the day
when you see without eyes
the golden ring
of Eternity.

Nuri's Swinging Song

Swing, oh swing, my little boat,
Swing, my darling boat!
Gently, like a silver dove
carry him, my only love
Swing, my darling boat

Grandeur is his golden crown
Beauty his embroidered gown
Swing, my darling boat

He is like the swan so white
feeds on pearls, and drinks their light
Swing, my darling boat

All the princes fold their hand
All the queens a-waiting stand
Swing, my darling boat

The gazelles so shy and fleet
put their heads upon their feet
Swing, my darling boat

When the arrows of his eye
cast their spells on low and high
Swing, my darling boat

Sing, ye birds in bush and tree,
Dance ye fishes in the sea!
Swing, my darling boat

In my hair, he made his bed,
On my breast there rests his head!
Swing, oh swing, my little boat,
Swing, my darling boat!

Sur Samundi

(as sung by Allan Faqir)

Sleep my beloved,
Dream my beloved,
dream of the endless sea of God

Allah —

Slowly, ye rivers
gently, ye waves —
all water flows to the endless sea
Deep are the rivers
deeper my longing
tears are the pearls in the endless sea.

Allah —

Are you a seagull?
Are you a foam-flake
light as a dream in the autumn wind?
Are you the fragrance
of a green island
far far away in the eastern light?

Allah —

Years passed like rain clouds
while I was waiting,
longing to cross yonder endless sea
Love was the rainbow
over the waves
into the heart of the endless sea.

Allah —

Sleep my beloved,
Dream my beloved,
Dream of the endless sea of God.

97

Dream waves
　　longing
　　sleep oh my soul —
　　　dream
　　dream oh my heart
　　　in
　　　　　　　God...
Allah —
　　　Allah —

Silent Talk

I talk to you
or do I talk to my soul?
I talk —
           there is no one to hear
and yet, I know, I am heard.

Day after day
you wander, and sing in my veins
Night after night
in the street of my nerves.

Words —
scent of a musk deer
           lost in the steppes of despair
Words —
pearls in a cloud's ear
           lost in the sunset of hope,
nightingales under the snow.

Postscript

These poems were written between 1974 and 1994, inspired, to a large extent, by the traditions of Islamic mystical poetry, in the first instance by Maulana Jalaluddin Rumi's work. Others reflect the mood of the folktales of Pakistan, mainly the Sindhi tradition, in which ages old tales were used by the poets of the Lower Indus Valley to symbolize the experiences of the loving soul. Again, others try to cope with life in the West, with journeys and wanderings through different landscapes, and in particular living in India and Pakistan. In order to facilitate the reading a number of brief notes on names and themes are given below; but we do hope that the poems will speak for themselves even without detailed explanations or commentaries about their literary or real background. About half of them were published in 1978 under the title *Mirror of an Eastern Moon* by East-West Publications, London – The Hague.

The People and Places

Adam, a young hero in the North-Western Frontier of the Indian Subcontinent who was deprived of his beloved Durkhana and died from grief; she, too, withered away in her longing for him.

Akbar, third Mughal emperor, ruled 1556 – 1605, built Fatehpur Sikri as memorial for Shaikh Salim Chishti, thanks to whose prayer his son Jahangir was born.

Aurangzeb, Akbar's great-grandson, ruled 1658 – 1707 after killing his three brothers; noted for his religious zeal.

Baba Rishi, Kashmiri saint of the 16th century, buried in Gulmarg.

Babur, founder of the Mughal Empire in India (1526 – 1530), is buried in Kabul.

Bullhe Shah, ecstatic poet in Panjabi; died 1758 in Qasur, Punjab.

Bidar, capital of the Bahmani kingdom of the Deccan from 1422 to the late fifteenth century.

Bijapur, capital of the Adilshahi dynasty of the Deccan (1495 – 1686).

Dewa Sharif, a Chishti sanctuary east of Lucknow.

Farhad, legendary Persian architect who fell in love with the Armenian princess Shirin, dug a canal through a rock to bring the milk of Shirin's cows to the valley, and died on hearing the false news of her death.

Fatehpur Sikri, the residence of the Mughal Emperor Akbar, from 1571 to 1586.

Fayzabad, the old capital of Awadh (Oudh), east of Lucknow.

Ganj ul -'ilm, Sufi saint and writer, died 1393 in Bijapur.

Ghazni, during the eleventh and twelfth centuries the cultural center of eastern Iran (Afghanistan), home of the mystical poet Sana'i (d. 1131).

Golconda, a city on the trade route between the eastern and the western coast of India, capital of the Qutbshahi kings (1512 – 1687), centre of the diamond trade.

Jalaluddin Rumi (1207 - 1273), the greatest mystical writer in the Persian tongue; born in the area of Balkh, Afghani-stan, he spent most of his life in Konya in Anatolia (the country called *Rum*, Byzantium – hence, his surname Rumi). His poetical work contains nearly 40,000 lyrical and more than 25,000 didactic verses as well as prose writing. He inspired the Sufi Order of the Whirling Dervishes.

Gwalior (India), famous for its fortress (often used as prison), for the tomb of Akbar's court singer Tansen, and for the magnificent mausoleum of the Sufi saint Muham-mad Ghauth Gwaliori (d. 1562), the author of a mystico-magical work, the Five Jewels.

Heer, heroine of a Panjabi folktale, falls in love with Ranjha on hearing his flute, and after many adventures is poisoned by her family.

Khankhanan Abdur Rahim, Akbar's and Jahangir's gener-alissimo, greatest patron of Persian and Hindi poets, and owner of the best library in India. Poet in Persian, Turki, and Hindi, he died in 1627.

Khidr, prototype of saintliness, drank from the Water of Life, which is hidden in the darkness, and is considered to be the immortal guide of the wayfarers in their quest for God.

Khuldabad, large cemetery near Daulatabad (Deccan).

Kichhauchha, east of Fayzabad, shrine of the Kubrawi saint Ashraf Jahangir (d. 1405 or 1425), a place haunted by evil spirits, and visited by mentally deranged people who hope for healing.

Konya, the old Iconium, in central Anatolia, centre of the Seljukid Empire of Anatolia from the twelfth to thirteenth centuries; contains Maulana Rumi's mausoleum, the "Green Dome."

Kotah, Rajput principality in India, noted for a special style of painting.

Layla, the beloved of Majnun.

Lila Chanesar, Sindhi folktale about a princess who bartered her husband away to her rival for a precious diamond necklace, and was duly punished.

Mahmud Gawan, Persian minister at the Bahmanid court of Bidar, de facto ruler from 1460 to 1487; assassinated by his rivals, and buried in the wilderness.

Mansoor, Husain ibn Mansur al-Hallaj, the martyr of mystical love, who was executed in Baghdad in 922, and became the symbol of mystical union through death.

Marib, centre of the kingdom of the Queen of Sheba, Bilqis, site of a famous dam.

Marui, Sindhi village girl who, kidnapped by Omar of Omarkot, remained faithful to her friends in the village; symbol of love of one's country and of the longing for the First Beloved.

Momal Rano, Sindhi tale of a woman who lost her beloved due to her own heedlessness and had to undergo long sufferings until she found him in her own heart.

Multan, a city at the southern edge of the Punjab, centre of the Suhrawardi Order from the early thirteenth century.

Mumtaz Mahal, Shah Jahan's favorite wife, who died in Burhanpur at the birth of her fourteenth child, and in whose memory the Taj Mahal was erected.

Majnun, "the demented," Layla's lover; wandering in the

desert he saw his beloved everywhere without needing her physical presence.

Nadira Begum, wife of the heir apparent to the Mughal Empire, Dara Shikoh, died in 1658 and is buried near the saint Mian Mir in Lahore; her husband was executed in 1659 by Dara Shikoh's brother Aurangzeb.

Neshat, lake near Srinagar (Kashmir).

Nuri, Sindhi fishermaid, who became the consort of Prince Tamachi thanks to her perfect obedience and humility.

Nurjahan, Persian wife of Emperor Jahangir (d. 1627), she built his mausoleum in Lahore and died in 1645 to be buried in a modest tomb.

Qasur, town in the Punjab close to the Indian border, centre of the admirers of the poet Bullhe Shah.

Rudauli Sharif, Chishti Sufi sanctuary east of Lucknow.

Saifulmuluk, a lake in Kaghan Valley; its name is connected with the story of Prince Saifulmuluk and the fairy Badi'ul–jamal.

Sassi, heroine of a Sindhi-Panjabi folktale; the adopted daughter of a washerman, attracted by her beauty even Punhun, the Prince of Kech in Balochistan; his relatives carried him away while she was asleep, and she died, seeking him in the deserts and mountains.

Shalimar, Mughal garden in Lahore, built under Shah Jahan around 1640.

Shams, Maulana Rumi's spiritual guide and mystical beloved, the "Sun of Tabriz."

Shirin, Armenian princess, loved by Farhad the mountain digger, and by Prince Khusrau.

Sohni, a Sindhi-Panjabi heroine who, married to an unloved man, swam every night through the Indus (or Chenab) to meet with her beloved Mehanval; one night her sister-in-law replaced the pot she used as lifebuoy by a vessel of unbaked clay which dissolved so that she died in the river.

Sorathi, Sindhi legend about King Diyach of Girnar (Gujarat), who offered his head to a singing minstrel, sacrificing his life for the sake of heavenly love.

Ucch Sharif, a city south-east of Multan near the Panjnad, centre of the Suhrawardiyya and the Qadiriyya Orders, adorned with some beautiful buildings with exquisite tilework.

Yusuf, the biblical Joseph, paragon of beauty, with whom Zulaykha fell in love. Yusuf's remark in the third stanza of the poem "Yusuf's Letter to Zulaykha" (p. 23) is based on Koran XII: 53.

Zulaykha, the Egyptian lady who fell in love with her husband's slave Yusuf.